Habit Building

How To Build Good Habits to Transform Your Life and Create Lasting Change without Feeling Overwhelmed and Frustrated

Your Free Gift

As a way of thanking you for the purchase, I'd like to offer you a complimentary gift:

- **5 Pillar Life Transformation Checklist:** This short book is about life transformation, presented in bit size pieces for easy implementation. I believe that without such a checklist, you are likely to have a hard time implementing anything in this book and any other thing you set out to do religiously and sticking to it for the long haul. It doesn't matter whether your goals relate to weight loss, relationships, personal finance, investing, personal development, improving communication in your family, your overall health, finances, improving your sex life, resolving issues in your relationship, fighting PMS successfully, investing, running a successful business, traveling etc. With a checklist like this one, you can bet that anything you do will seem a lot easier to implement until the end. Therefore, even if you don't continue reading this book, at least read the one thing that will help you in every other aspect of your life. Grab your copy now by clicking/tapping here or simply enter http://bit.ly/2fantonfreebie into your browser. Your life will never be the same again (if you implement what's in this book), I promise.

PS: I'd like your feedback. If you are happy with this book, please leave a review on Amazon

Introduction

In your quest to actualize your life's dreams, you may be driving yourself too hard without even realizing it and unaware that working yourself to the bone does not guarantee that you will accomplish all the things you have set out to accomplish nor does it ensure that all your juicy dreams come true.

If you have been living with the wrong set of habits and daily routines, it is only a matter of time before they start taking their toll on your health, state of mind, and focus. It is impossible to talk about your life, achievements, and success without talking about your habits. This is because your habits are undoubtedly the sole determinants of what you achieve or fail to achieve in life.

Someone may beg to differ with this assertion citing other powerful factors such as time management, setting the right priorities, never giving up, shunning distractions, working diligently and other such factors. These factors do play a role in your overall success. However, a cursory look at all these other important factors that help define your success will still point your attention back to your habits because every one of these important factors directly or indirectly relates to a set of habits you have already cultivated.

To achieve success, therefore, you need to have the right sets of habits. You need build habits that stick and come automatically without any conscious effort on your part.

This book is going to help you learn 15 seasoned steps you can take to effect the desired positive changes you need without the frustrating failures that always follow habits and lifestyle change efforts.

Table of Contents

Understanding Habits and Their Power

As powerful and influential as habits are to your life, and inasmuch as you would love to know how they form and how you can break them, there is no single one-fits-all formula for breaking old habits and building new ones in their place. When it comes to habit breakage and formation, over a thousand formulas and theories exist with all of them based on different factors.

Habits differ in the same way one individual differs from another. Curbing your overeating habits is not and cannot be the same thing as quitting smoking; changing how you react to issues in your relationship is not the same thing as learning to beat the habit of procrastination or learning to prioritize tasks in your place of work in their order of importance.

Each habit has specific driving cravings much like how different neurological, biological, physical, and environmental factors influence each individual. However, going by the results of several available researches, there seems to be a neurological loop at the core of every new habit formation. A loop made of a cue, a routine, and a reward.

To understand your own habits, you need to identify the components of your own neurological loops. After diagnosing the habit loop of any particular behavior you have been exhibiting, you can then look for new ways of successfully and positively supplanting old vices with new routines.

The next step talks about how the habit neurological loop works and how it can work for you:

Step 1: Understand the Habits Neurological Loop and Make It Work for You

Before becoming an effortless routine you can do repeatedly without thinking about, each habit begins as a conscious effort.

Every habit has three parts—together called the habit loop. These are a cue**,** a ***routine/behavior***, and a ***reward***. Understanding how this loop works and interrupting it is the key to breaking any negative habit you wish to do away with. Understanding how the habit loop works is also the key to building the new habits you need to make the changes you wish to make in all areas of your life.

Think about a particular thing that was very difficult for you to learn, one that took you a very long time to master—like how to parallel park. At first, parallel parking probably seemed like one of the most difficult tasks in life, but because you wanted to master it, you devoted lots of time and mental energy to ensure you master it. However, the moment you began to do it without the initial struggles and clumsiness, it became easier—almost something habitual.

Every other habit such as brushing your teeth, gambling, riding a bike, driving a car, etc. follows the same neurological and behavioral pattern:

How Habits Form

According to results from several scientific researches aimed at unraveling how habits form, every habit begins with a psychological pattern called a *habit loop*. The habit loop consists of first, a trigger—often referred to as the cue—that tells your brain to go into some kind of automatic mode and allow a new behavior to form. Then there is a second component called the routine, which happens to be the behavior itself. Then there is a third part called the reward: something the brain craves and that helps it remember the habit loop before the repetition of the process that makes up a particular habit.

Some neuroscientists have managed to trace the habit-making behavior to a particular part of our brain called the basal ganglia, a part that also plays a vital role in pattern recognitions, development, emotions, and memories. However, the decisions you make happen in a part of your brain called the prefrontal cortex. The moment a behavior becomes a habit, the decision-making part of your brain goes into some sort of sleep mode whenever you are acting out the habit in question.

Actually, when you are acting out a behavior that has become habitual and automatic, your brain seems to limit computing power since it is not necessary. This is an advantage because when it happens, it means you can channel the whole of your brain activities to something else even while engaged in that habit. This explains why you can be driving, pedaling, or riding a bike and still be engaged in something else such as listening to music, interacting with someone, etc.

You can do these and other complex behavior without giving them any conscious attention or thought because the capacity of your basal ganglia allows you take a behavior and turn it into an automatic routine.

How to Make the Neurological Loop Work for You

One important point worthy of note here is that certain factors such as timing, environment, emotions, and the people around you influence your habits. When any or some of these influential factors change, your habits are likely to change too. This is why taking a vacation is a good way to break some old habits or redesign them into useful one.

For instance, take the way you have been brushing your teeth, taking your morning shower, arranging your shoes, or pulling out of your driveway at home. You will do any of these things the exact same way without thinking about them. However, the moment your environment changes, the cues are most likely to change and the patterns/routines will change to reflect this.

This is why it is advisable to try breaking negative habits such as smoking while on vacation: because the mental cues for such habits, cues such as the friends that trigger your urge to drink or smoke will no longer be there. Once the cues are no longer there, you can easily find a more positive habit to build in their place and still enjoy the satisfying rewards they bring you.

If vacationing is out of the question depending on what you do and where you live, you can change your environment, move homes, change your circle of friends, the places you hang out, or even change your daily routines. This will help you break the neurological loop and pave the way for building new habits.

Next, we will see how you can change your mindset to change your life:

Step 2: Increase Your Chances of Success by Effecting a Change of Mindset

What is mindset?

Before we go into how you change your life by changing your mindset, it is very important that you understand what mindset is as well as its connection to your habits.

We can define your mindset as the sum of your knowledge, which includes your beliefs and thoughts about the world and your life in general. Your mindset is solely responsible for how you receive and react to information and situations. It acts as a filter for whatever goes in and out of your mind.

Different people have different sets of mindset. This explains why we can hear the same thing and interpret it in different ways. When going for anything in life, you need to have the right mindset because the mindset you hold greatly determines the results you get.

Developing the right mindset is the right way to learning every new thing you wish to learn such as a new set of habits. Your mindset forms your belief system and in turn, your belief system influences your habits and behaviors.

Developing the right mindset is the first step to building new habits and changing your life.

How to Change Your Mindset and Life

To change your mindset and change your life, take these steps:

1: Always look for the right information

The world thrives on information, which is why we have lots of information about everything. Always make sure you have the most accurate information because having this information helps shape your mindset about any particular issue. This is also applicable when working on overcoming a certain habit such as procrastination.

The internet has loads of information on how to beat procrastination. However, more than 90% of this information will not yield any substantive results, which is why you should ensure you only read reliable sources of information such as great books, authority blogs, and some top quality information products. When you have the right information from the right source, you will build your mindset on the right foundation and get the changes you desire.

2: Get a role model

There are people in your field who have done what you wish to do and some who have overcome the bad habits you are fighting to overcome. Find such people, and find a way to stay close to them. Learn what they do and how they do the things they do; learn the habits they live with and their daily routines.

Follow what they do and what they say, and you will have their kind of mindset and see the positive changes you want in your life taking shape before your eyes. You cannot go wrong following the habits of a role model who has made a success of his life and career with those same set of habits.

Of course, some of such successful people might still have one or two vices they are battling with; you do not have to pick up the negatives along with the positives. Take what you need for your journey and discard the rest.

3: Put your current beliefs on a pedestal

Look at your present mindset by re-examining your belief-system. Are these beliefs supportive of the life you wish to live or have they been dragging you backwards and limiting you? The thing about beliefs is that they can help you succeed or make you fail without your notice: they remain domiciled in your subconscious region.

To unmask your belief system, you need to ask yourself certain relevant questions such as what you wish to achieve in your life, what you wish to become, where you wish to be in the next 5-10 years or more, what is standing in your way to achieving these dreams right now, etc.

You can change your negative beliefs by declaring supportive positive statements on such beliefs. These supportive beliefs birthed by these positive statements are easy to internalize by making positive affirmations a daily habit and routine.

4: Coin specific visions and goals to shape your mindset

One very proactive way to build your mindset is to see where you wish to go through clearly defined goals and visions about the future. This will help you know the right habits to build and which ones to discard.

Practicing visualization will help you here. Imagining the future you desire in images and colorful motion pictures will help your mindset and habits conform to the beautiful vision you have about the future. You can then break down that beautiful vision into feasible daily, weekly, biweekly, monthly, yearly goals.

5: Define your purpose

It is important to know what your life is about and what you can contribute to make the world a better place. There is something—a talent, a great skill—something unique you carry that sets you apart from everyone else. The sooner you find that which makes you unique and special, the sooner you achieve a mental shift for the right habits you need to fulfill destiny to form and stick.

Here are a few questions you need to ask yourself to help you discover the "you in you"

- What do you love doing?

- What are you very good at?

- What problem can you help the world solve with your hands?

- What cause do you feel like giving your life towards? Whatever your conscience is directing you shows where your spirit is.

Following these steps to define who you are will help you find your unique voice and unique thing you can do to make the world a different place because you are who you are and no one else can be who you are better than you can. Connecting with your purpose is a great way to develop a success mindset and build success habits you need succeed.

6: Keep your mindset protected at all times

Building the right mindset is not enough. You also need to protect your mindset against negative influences from people, experiences, and your environment. You need to protect it against wrong information. Protecting your mindset against negativities helps keep your confidence in place, and with that, you can build any new positive habit without qualms.

Let us see now look at how keystone habits that can change every area of your life:

Step 3: Effect Positive Change in All Areas of Your Life Using This Keystone Habit

Some habits are so powerful that making them a part of your success habits can cause a positive change in virtually every area of your life. Imagine building one keystone habit that can change the tempo of your relationship with your spouse, make you a better parent, give you more time to exercise, increase your job productivity, and boost your health and happiness all in one swift swoop.

While it might seem most unlikely that one habit can help you achieve so much positive results, some habits are actually that powerful. Before we go any further, let us cultivate an understanding of what keystone habits are.

What Are Keystone Habits?

Keystone habits are the all-powerful and influential habits that can help you build every other positive habit you need to succeed in all areas of your life. Keystone habits lead to the development of a chain of other positive habits. Their formation starts a chain effect in every area of your life that can lead to very visible positive effects.

In this guide, we shall discuss keystone habits you can build to help you see the change you desire in every aspect of your life:

1: Develop a Healthy Sleep Habit as Your Keystone Habit

When we talk about good sleep habit, a number of things come into play here. A good and healthy sleeping habit spans across when you sleep, how you sleep, the duration of your sleep, and various other factors.

We will look into each of these components of a good sleep habit and all other healthy habits this keystone habit can help you develop to effect very positive changes in all areas of your life.

Deal with every habit that makes you go to bed late first

It is always good to start dealing with issues from their roots. A number of habits you have built overtime can keep you awake all night and rob you of your night sleep. The first step you must take towards building the keystone habit of developing a healthy sleep habit is to do away with every counter habit that makes it hard for you to stick to your bedtime routine.

Factors such as watching late night movies, TV shows, playing video games, surfing the internet, chatting with someone dear on social media, etc., are among negative habits that can affect the way and when you sleep.

Commit to sleeping at least 8 hours every night

According to medical practitioners, a healthy adult should get at least 8 hours of sleep per night for the body to get the adequate rests it needs to carry out all of its functions. However, sleeping 8 hours will not happen automatically; it needs conscious work to make it happen.

Here are a few steps you can take to ensure you get a peaceful 8-hour sleep every night:

- **Have a specific time for retiring to bed every night:** It is easier to commit to a daily sleep schedule when you have a specific time when you wind up the day's activities and retire to bed. If you do this consistently every night, your brain will automatically learn to shut down all mental and bodily functions once it is the hour you have chosen for your night sleep to enable you enjoy the night rest your body so much craves.

- **Plan your day well and make room for emergencies:** No matter how well you plan your day, unforeseen emergencies such as a robbery attack, a health emergency, fire outbreak, natural disaster, or family feud can disorganize all your plans. The best way to ensure your daily plans do not scuttle so much that they affect your sleep is to leave room for such emergencies and plan to attend to them as soon as possible.

- **Shun all late night activities:** We mentioned the need to deal with your negative habits that keep you up late every night. Whatever you do that keeps you awake when you should be sleeping is not in your best interests as depriving your body of sleep will have very serious health effects eventually. Schedule a better time to go through those emails and reply to your messages on social media. Schedule a time for gossiping with your spouse or flat mates other than the late night hours, and if you must use of the night hours, know when to excuse yourself and retire to bed.

- **Develop healthy habits that help you enjoy a good night rest without interruptions:** Always turn the bedroom lights off once it is your bedtime as leaving the lights on might deceive your brain into believing it is still day. Discover what helps you sleep well and use it to your advantage. It could be soft soulful music, it could be a particular sleeping position, or it could a physical workout or meditation. Whatever it is, make sure you utilize its power to help you get uninterrupted sleep every night. You may need to experiment with some of these things to be sure what works for you.

How Adequate Sleep Changes All Areas of Your Life

How does developing the keystone habit of getting adequate sleep per night help you develop other important habits you need to change your life in every way?

Let us look at some common examples:

- **Helps you become an early riser:** Becoming an early riser is a great success on its own as it gives you the time you need to enjoy mindful breakfast with your family, engage in the morning workout you need to stay healthy, and the mindful meditation you need to maintain mental clarity.

- **Keeps you energized and refreshed enough to work out:** The benefits of any morning workout are not something you should take lightly. Going to bed early and rising early helps you do all those exercises you need to do daily to maintain your body fitness and flexibility.

- **You can enjoy a mindful, healthy breakfast:** Sleeping early and rising early will help you take your time while you enjoy your breakfast. Instead of rushing through breakfast and eating whatever is available, you can now pay more attention to what you eat and how they affect your body; this will in turn help you stay in shape and maintain optimum health.

- **Helps you spend more time with your loved ones:** Spending time with your loved ones is among the easily ignored success habits that can give you the motivation you need to go after your dreams and daily goals with everything you have. Becoming an early riser will help you spend some early morning time with your spouse, kids, and siblings. This is one way you can bond with your loved ones. You can decide to engage in any productive activity with your loved ones such as reading something positive, watching or listening to a motivating clip, exercising together, etc.

This single keystone habit—and all other habits that come along with it—will help you make daily progress in all areas of your life even when you are tired or behind schedule.

Let us now discuss some habits you need to adopt to make daily progress in all areas of your life:

Step 4: Make Daily Progress in Your Life Even When You Are Behind Deadline or Tired

Contrary to popular belief, it is actually possible to make daily progress in all aspects of your life irrespective of obvious obstructions and setbacks. All you need is a good plan and the right set of habits.

Some people believe those who move ahead of others are just lucky, but the truth remains that those "lucky" ones have learnt how to plan their lives and prepare for each day before it dawns armed with the right set of habits when opportunity comes calling.

Here, we shall look into the habits you need to adopt to make daily progress in your life and steps you can take to make them part of your daily life.

Know the People in Your Life

Knowing the people in your life involves going beyond the obvious details about them. You need to pay close attention to what they like, what makes them tick, their major values and aspirations. This will help you know when and how to be more useful to them.

Everyone likes to have someone around him who understands him and what his life is about. Once you get close enough, you will learn what most others do not know about these people and they can feel comfortable enough to bring you into their confidence when it comes to certain important issues.

This habit will help you get ahead in school, at work, and elsewhere. Even if your classmates or colleagues see it as brown-nosing, do what you have to do to get closer to your boss or professor as this will help you get ahead more easily.

Become Better At Communication

Good communication skills will help you get help when you need it. A good manner of approach may be all you need to get the right people to help you pull off difficult tasks.

No one came into this world a great communicator; great communication is a skill we all learn somewhere in our journey. Even the greatest of all orators we have today had to learn to communicate better at some point in their career. Even if you do not have any business with public speaking or public life, enhancing your communication skills will sure help you pass important messages when there is need to even without saying anything.

Moreover, communication plays very vital roles in relationships and the more you are able to communicate well with your spouse, the more your chances of sustaining your business and private relationships.

To improve your communication skills, you can dedicate some time daily to learning the basics of body languages and facial expressions and their meanings. In addition, learn to listen more than you talk during conversations—this will help you pick up important points and learn new things to make daily progress.

Plan before Taking Action

If you are the type that undertakes tasks without giving them proper attention or having in place an adequate plan of action, there is a limit to what you can achieve daily. Do not be in a haste to begin when you obviously do not understand the specifics of a specific task.

It is better to spend time studying the job and learning what you need to pull it through before you begin any task than wasting the whole time on trials and error until you are tired and behind deadlines. Adequate planning and paying proper attention to details will ensure you never miss a deadline in your line of work.

Form the Habit of Undertaking Tasks One at a Time

If you are not among those few who are highly talented and can take up several tasks at once, do not take on more tasks than you can handle at any given time. Taking the one-at-a-time approach will help you get a lot done in less time. It is far better to complete a few things well within the time allotted to you than to try to do so many things at the same time and fail.

With a few tasks, you can be sure to approach tasks with better clarity of mind, which enhances your chances of pulling off any project and meeting deadlines.

Ask For Help When You Need It

Do not be one of those self-sufficient people who believe they do not need the help of anybody to complete tasks. No matter how good you are at what you do, there will always come some days and some points when you could use an input from someone else. A tree, they say, has never and can never make a forest so make sure you do not try to be an island unto yourself especially when it is obvious you are running behind schedule.

Ask for help even if you have to pay for the help or share the credit for the accomplished task. Why miss a vital goal for your team because you want your name on the scorer's list when you can easily pass the ball to a nearby teammate to help you push the ball into the opponents net? Two, they say, are better than one; so be guided.

Learn to Begin Early

We talked about going to bed early and rising early as a keystone habit and the several other positive habits that this keystone habit helps you develop. One of the important benefits of such habits is to get to work earlier; beginning early is a sure way to accomplish much on time before your energy begins to sag. If you want to get a lot done during the day, make it a habit to start your day early.

You cannot get ahead if you do not start ahead of everyone. Developing this habit will ensure you never miss any deadlines ever again. Actually, when you start early, you will be able to deliver jobs before the stipulated deadlines, which is good for your business reputation.

Learn To Take Immediate Action

People who keep waiting for the storm to clear never get anything done because life runs in such a way that storms go in turns. There is no such thing as the perfect time and condition. Those who wait for the best time end up waiting forever and never get anything done.

Start as soon as the idea hits your mind. Start as soon as the time for the task starts ticking. Start as soon as the commencement gunshot goes off. There is no point waiting. Start now or you will fall by the roadside, arrive late, and miss the coveted prize.

Let us now look at steps you can take to master the habit formation loop and hook on to your new habits more easily:

Step 5: Master the Habit Formation Loop and Use It to Hook onto Your New Habits

We have mentioned the habit formation loop a number of times, but it is important learn we get deeper insight into how this loop works and how you can use it to internalize any new habit and make it stick.

We have plenty of tools out there that can help you break your negative habits and build new ones in their place. However, the best way to master your habits and their formation is to understand the mental process behind their formation. This mental process is what we commonly refer to as the habit loop. The belief is that the main key to breaking every bad habit in to trick yourself into swapping the negative habit you want to break with something more positive you want to make a habit.

The habit loop on its own is a very straightforward process: you receive some kind of cue, you address the cue you receive through some behavior known as the routine, and then you reap the reward of that behavior. Many people who try to overcome negative behaviors fail because they try to remove the cue and the reward without paying any attention to the routine.

The best way to overcome your negative habits is to learn how you can implement a positive habit to give you the same rewards you get from the negative habit you have been trying to overcome. For example, let us say you want to go out with your coworkers at the end of a long day at work to enjoy a few drinks. In this case, there are actually positive rewards that come from this habit:

- The socializing that occurs inevitably

- The relaxing effects of the alcohol on your body and your nervous system

We can say that these two rewards are valid and necessary. If you quit drinking without replacing it with any other habit that can help you feel good and relaxed, and that can satisfy your socializing cravings, you will likely be a very unhappy person. The trick here is to make sure you keep the cue (a feeling of tiredness, boredom, loneliness) and the rewards (socializing, relaxation, boosting your feel good hormones) while replacing the routine or behavior that helps you get the rewards your body so much craves.

This goes on to show that the major key to changing this negative habit in not in giving up going out with your colleagues and socializing when you are tired or bored. If you do that, you will end up making yourself unhappy and separating yourself from your colleagues, which makes it very likely for you to slide right back into that same habit you want to ditch.

The right step to take here is to find out which of the colleagues you have been drinking with who will probably be in need of a lifestyle change and get him to join you in some other activity that will help you relax and socialize. You can try yoga classes, go rock-climbing, volunteer for some non-profit outdoor activities, etc. The key is to fix the routine or behavior without trying to tamper with any other element of the routine.

Let us help you learn one strategy that can help you stick to your daily routines and achieve your daily goals faster.

Step 6: Master A Strategy That Can Help You Stick To Your Daily Goals and Routines

You cannot just expect your new habits to stick without a clearly thought out plan. You can achieve your daily goals and stick to your daily routines if you have a daily plan to help you do so, and sticking to such new routines for long will help your new habits form and become a part of your life for as long as you live.

Here are some steps you can take to help you stick to your daily routines:

Be specific

To stick to your daily routines and achieve your daily goals, you need to be specific with your plans. When you have very vague plans, such plans can easily slip through cracks. In addition, such plans are easy to forget or seem uninteresting.

For instance, let us say you want to add more daily reading time into your daily schedule and timetable. That is a great goal but it is unlikely that you will get any results with such vague goals unless your become specific. You should clearly define what extra materials you are going to be reading in the extra reading time you have added. Do you wish to read just to be entertained? Are you reading to do away with some free time or are you reading to be educated? You should clearly define why you are reading more.

If you are reading to be educated, what exactly do you wish to learn? Be sure to know what you wish to learn each day of the week and for how long. Also, be specific about what steps you wish to take to avoid any distractions during the time you have allotted to your extra daily reading. Where will this reading take place? Will it happen in the study, bedroom, or attic? Be specific about the reading location. You should be specific about each of these points while making your plans.

Use this approach for every other daily routine you wish to build into a habit.

Devise a means to stay motivated all day

It is common to find yourself in a situation where the very things you wish to make a part of your daily routines are the things you have no interest in and therefore lack the natural motivation to engage in. In such situation, constantly remind yourself why you are adopting this new routine, habit, or setting this new goal.

Always remind yourself why you need to stick to that new eating habit, why you need to go to bed early and rise early, why you must not miss your daily workout for anything in the world, why you must not drink with those friends anymore, etc.

Constantly reminding yourself of the why of the new habit or routine is one way to ensure you stay motivated all day long. Another great way to stay motivated is to read a book that helps you understand your goal. You can do some research to learn more about what you plan to do and how best you can ensure you stay on track.

Create a checklist

You need to list out the tasks you wish to accomplish in your daily routine. This checklist will help you remember what you need to do daily to stick to your daily routine and achieve your daily goals until that routine has become a habit. Always consult your checklist to rule out what you have accomplished and to remind yourself what comes next after the task you have completed.

Maintain a daily log

You need to monitor your progress every step of the way. This will help you see how well you are doing, how effective the routines you have chosen are, and if you are on the right track to achieving your daily goals. Doing this is another great way of knowing what is not working for your routines and daily goals so that you can necessary changes in approach to achieve better results.

Sticking to your routine once you have planned it out becomes a whole lot easier when you keep a daily journal. Making your routine is never going to be easy, but the moment you implement the points and ideas here, it will not be long before you start seeing the results you desire, and your routines can easily become your success habits.

Let us see how a token economy can help you reinforce your new habits:

Step 7: Set Up a Token Economy to Reinforce Your New Positive Habits

What is a token economy?

A token economy is a system of contingency management based on the systematic reinforcement of a target behavior or habit. The reinforcers used to reinforce the target behaviors are what we call symbols or tokens that we can exchange for other reinforcers or a more valuable reward.

Every token economy draws on the principles of behavioral economics and operant conditioning and you can thus situate it within an applied behavioral analysis. Token economies can work on both adults and children.

Here, we will help you understand how you can build your own token economy to help reinforce your new positive habits.

How to Use a Token Economy to Reinforce a New Habit

As the name implies, a token has no real value on its own, and therefore, you must exchange it with habit reinforcers such as a reward you enjoy, which could be an activity, a visit to somewhere cozy, seeing your favorite sitcom for 30-60 minutes, visiting your favorite restaurant and enjoying your favorite dish, etc.

When using a token economy to motivate yourself into sticking to a new habit, your main goal should be to find a reward that makes so much sense that you think it is worth earning. Using a token economy is however easier when you are using it to reinforce positive behaviors in others than it is when you are using it on yourself.

Take for instance a scenario where you want to stop biting your fingernails, quit smoking, or quit any other negative habit. Assume this habit has been with you for as long as you can remember and everything you have used to try to quit the habit so far has failed, here is what to do to make the token economy approach work for you:

Grab a calendar, mark off your takeoff date and your first milestone/reward date. Since it the belief is that quitting an old habit or developing any new habit takes at least 3 days, you should make 3 weeks your first milestone and reward date.

You earn a number of points you have chosen each day you did not engage in the negative habit you wish to drop or engage in the positive habit you wish to build. If you engage in that negative habit during the day, you lose some points until you are down to no point. This will help you stay away from the habit all through the day since you will not want to miss the reward you can exchange for your points.

Calculate the number of points you will earn within the 3-weeks period and stipulate what reward is due to that number of points when you reach it. If it takes you longer than the three weeks to reach that number of points, it means you missed the first milestone, but that should not discourage you. If, for instance, you are to earn 5 points per day for 21 days, that will be 105 points. You can decide to go give yourself a treat of your favorite dish at your favorite restaurant, buy yourself a beautiful gift, visit somewhere you have been planning to visit, etc.

Let us see how reviewing and changing your approach will help you get better results with your habits and approaches:

Step 8: Review and Readjust Your Approach Periodically

While working to make any habit or routine stick, it is important to make room for periodical reviews of your approach as a way to help you know when to make necessary adjustments.

No approach is perfect on its own, which explains why periodical reviews are of utmost importance. These reviews will help you glance back at yourself when you were still holding on to your old habits and the you after you have started living with new daily goals, habits, and routines.

These reviews will help you see where you are making progress and strategies that are producing the exact results you wish to see in different areas of your life. In addition, these periodical reviews will help you see where and when you need to drop your old approach and infuse new techniques to help you achieve your daily goals and make your new habits stick.

Here are steps you can take:

• Recall how the old habits you dropped affected your life. Think about that habit you replaced with the new one and recall how it messed up your life.

- Compare the life you live now to the old you. In which ways has your new habits and approaches changed the quality of your life? How has waking up early to engage in your early morning workouts made you a healthier and happier person? How has getting rid of unnecessary friends and tasks helped you spend more time with people that matter the most in your life? This evaluation will help you see if your new habits, goals, and approaches are worth it and in line with your big picture.

- Is there a better way you could have done things or a better approach you could have adopted to get better results?

- Experiment with new ideas and approaches and see how well they fit into your new lifestyle and visions.

Let us see how habits activation energy effects your habits and how you can use it to make your new habits stick:

Step 9: Change Your Habits' Activation Energy

What is activation energy?

In case you are wondering what activation has to do with your habits, it is important you understand what activation energy is all about.

Activation energy is a very popular term in the field of chemistry and biochemistry, but if you have had nothing to do with these fields in your high school and college years, you may not be able to understand a thing about what activation energy is or how it works.

In chemistry, activation energy is the energy you need to begin a reaction. For instance, a paper does not and will not automatically and spontaneously burn when exposed to air; a certain amount of heat in necessary before the paper can burst into flames.

The moment the paper starts burning, the reaction has all it takes to sustain itself without further heating. This is because the burning molecules releases enough energy to push every surrounding molecule over the edge and get them burning with the others.

Getting Rid Of the Activation of Energy of Your Negative Habits

Assume you have a negative habit you would give anything to replace—like opening the fridge at interval and pulling out a bottle of your favorite beer. If you ensure no beer comes into your home, it becomes more difficult to get your hands on your favorite beer and makes it very unlikely that you will drink many bottles of beers a day until you can spend a whole day without drinking one bottle.

This is because you will have to drive out to a nearby store or beer parlor to buy that beer, and thus, the activation energy for that habit increases making it easier for you to quit the negative habit.

The same applies to your addiction to social media sites. If you delete all apps and shortcut icons to such platforms on your PC or smartphone, you will need to type in their full URL before logging into your accounts on sites like Facebook, Instagram, or Twitter. The increased activation energy will make you visit such sites less.

It is obvious that raising the activation energy of the habits you wish to stop works wonders when it comes to helping you quit every compulsive behavior that has turned into a negative habit. When it comes to your habits, it does not end here. The real power of activation energy lies in helping you build and internalize your new positive habits.

Increasing the Activation Energy for Your Good Habits

Since increasing the activation energy for your bad habits helps you quit them, lowering the activation energy for your new habits will help you do them more often.

Lowering the activation energy for your positive habits you want to stick requires shifting your mental focus from the task to something more trivial and easier to do. For instance, if you wish to build the habit of running for 30 minutes every morning, to reduce the activation energy required to get you on your feet and out of the house, shift your focus from the running and pay attention to putting on your running shoes and stepping out of the house.

Once you stand in front of your door, the rest will natural take care of itself. The same goes for other habits such as reading or writing. Do not focus on the entire book; focus on doing one chapter, then another, and another until you get to the conclusion page.

Steps to take:

- Pick one positive habit.

- Choose the easiest way to make the habit easier, smaller, or more fun.

- Focus all your attention and energy on doing that first small step and nothing more. Let the rest flow naturally. It is that simple. Try this now!

Let us see how having the right people around you can help you build new habits faster:

Step 10: Surround Yourself with Positive People Who Bring Out the Best in You

It makes no sense to make every effort to bring about the changes you desire in your life by dropping your negative habits and picking up new positive habits and have your efforts truncated by the wrong crowd you choose to have around you.

An important thing you should do that is in line with making your new routines and habits stick is to surround yourself with people whose journey and yours finds a common meeting point.

Below are points to help you pick the right people that can help you stick to your newfound positive routines and habits:

- **Start with your immediate circle:** You already have some positive people in your life who can help you stick with the new habits you have adopted. Look into your list of friends and get closer to your friends to know what they spend most of their daily time doing and what causes they spend their free time pursuing. This will help you know those who are committed to effecting the same type of changes you are working to see in your own life. You can find such people in your family, your class, your social circles, etc. Find a reason and ways to hang out with such people. Hanging out with the right kinds of people will help you find people that can keep you accountable.

- **Extend your network and make new friends:** Even if you do not find the right people in your immediate circle, you can extend your social tentacles and make some new friends. Chances are that you will find some positive-minded people who can help you reinforce the new habits you have built. Internalizing such newfound positive habits becomes easy when you have people who can always call you to order when you try to fall back to your old negative habit.

A commitment contract can take you far on your new habits' formation journey. Let us see how:

Step 11: Build a Commitment Contract

One other great way to ensure you stick to your new habits is to put your daily goals into writing and confirm them with someone who wants to see you succeed with your habit change. To make it easier for you to stick to the new habits you have built, you can attach a reward to every time you stick to your daily plans and a kind of penalty whenever you default.

For instance, you can commit to a contract to quit smoking within six months with a penalty for failing to stick to your no smoking decisions. This penalty could be something like losing about 6 months' worth of smoking money whenever you slide back into this habit within the stipulated period. You can donate this money to a charity of your choice or allow your referee to use it anyhow he/she deems fit.

Steps to take:

- **Stick to just one goal at a time:** You need to write down one goal and stay focused on achieving that goal rather than juggling between various goals.

- **Put down the necessary steps required to reach your daily goals:** The steps do not need to be anything complicated. All you need is something you can easily understand and do without any help.

- **Work with deadlines:** You can pick a day or a week as your deadline. This will help you change these goals whenever there is need for it to ensure you do not tie yourself down with any long-term contract.

- **Set rewards:** Whenever you achieve your daily or weekly goals, reward yourself handsomely to reinforce these positive habits and motivate yourself to do more.

Let us see how accountability can help you stick to your new habits:

Step 12: Use Accountability to Stick to Your Habit

Becoming accountable for your goals ensures you make new habits stick. Here are a few steps and ideas you can use to make accountability work for you and help you internalize your new habits.

- **Stay in the right frame of mind:** Knowing your why will go a long way to help you form new habits. Ask yourself why you want to form this new habit and how your new goal is important to you. Ask yourself how forming this new habit will help you live a better life. If your WHY is not strong enough, you will struggle to find the motivation to reinforce the new habit. If you do not find a lot of value in the new habit, you may never want to sacrifice a lot to form the new habit. Knowing your why and getting a stronger why if the old one is not strong enough will help you stay in the right mindset.

- **Make that habit a top priority:** You cannot stick to any new goal or habit until you organize your life well enough to get rid of all distractions and time wasters. This type of decluttering will help you get your priorities right and stick to what really matters most of the time. Plan your daily schedule in such a way that you will always have some free time to work on internalizing that new habit and learning whatever new technique you need to learn to make it easier for you to stick with your new habit and daily goals.

- **An accountability partner will help you stick to your new habits:** You can hardly go wrong with an accountability partner. It works better when you and your accountability partner look out for each other and hold each other accountable for your daily routines and new habits. If you stay committed to each other, your accountability partner will help you stay true to your routines until your habits stick. Make sure you find someone who is reliable and someone whose unbiased judgment you can count on.

- **Learn as much as you can about your goals and habits:** It helps to keep your mind nourished on the goals you wish to pursue and the new habits you wish to internalize. It is important that you find out all the ways the new habit will help you live a better life and become a better you. If you know how much your health and wellbeing will improve when you make mindful meditation and physical workout part of your daily routines and learn all their health and fitness benefits, it will help you stick to such positive habits for as long as you live.

Identifying mental loopholes and avoiding them at all cost will make your journey easier.

Step 13: Learn to Identify Mental Loopholes and Avoid Falling Into Them

Mental loopholes are the kind of negative mindsets and stereotypical way of thinking that are likely to discourage you from following your daily routines, pursuing your daily goals, and sticking to your new habits.

Follow these steps to avoid every mental loophole

- **Identify your mental loopholes:** The very first step you must take is to identify the mental blocks and loopholes that keep you from following through with your daily routines, goals, and new habits. What makes you think you cannot successfully achieve these goals? Perhaps you think you are not creative enough; perhaps you think you do not have all it takes when it comes to self-discipline and the willpower to persevere. Whatever it is, knowing what holds you back will help you know where to channel your fighting energies.

- **Develop a freewriting habit:** Freewriting is a technique used to change your thought patterns and escape the pitfalls presented by mental loopholes when working with new goals and habits. Simply open a new word doc. or pull out your writing paper and pen, and write whatever comes to mind. This will re-energize your thought process. Set out 15-20 minutes every day for this exercise. Write down your fears, your cares, and evaluate and counter them with positive lines of thoughts and affirmations. This technique also works when you are in need of new ideas.

- **Accomplish daily small wins to boost your self-confidence**: Your mental loophole could have to do with your self-perception, which shows you need to increase your self-confidence daily. One effective way to achieve this is to engage in small projects you can easily pull off daily. Small meaningful tasks like rearranging your bedroom, doing your laundry, sifting through your unread emails, doing the dishes, trimming the lawn yourself, and any other small task that will help you feel you have accomplished something new each day will help you escape mental loopholes.

- **Change the look of your work and homes pace:** The orderliness of where you live and where you work affects your mental stability and performance. Working in a neat environment will help you have a sharper mental focus, identify mental loopholes, avoid them and achieve your daily goals, and stick to your habits.

- **Learn how your role model escaped these mental loopholes:** If you have an authority figure you look up to or an accountability partner, you can talk about these loopholes and learn how they deal with such issues to learn a new technique you can use to stay in line.

There will be times when you will encounter some setbacks and failures even after applying these techniques, and it is important you know how best to handle such setbacks when they do occur.

Step 14: Learn To Limit the Negative Effects of Setbacks and Failures When They Do Occur

Failures and setbacks are all part of the success journey, and you cannot avoid them completely especially when building new habits and daily routines. Some of the steps we have outlined thus far will work without hitches, but some will require some patience and perseverance before you start seeing the results you desire.

Whenever you encounter any kind of setback, take these steps to limit their effects on your overall progress and results:

- **Accept you need to do more:** Changing your lifestyle, routines, and habits is not one of those things you can pull off without any setbacks. Remember you are trying to get rid of certain habits you have been living with for as long as you can remember. Some of these habits even come with some short-lived benefits, and it will therefore be wrong to expect yourself to detach yourself and your mind from them in one try. The first steps to turning your failures to success when you do not see the results you desire immediately is to accept you need to put in more time and effort to make the habits stick.

- **Change the way you see failure:** Failure is not as bad as we make it out to be. Failures and setbacks help you know what works and what does not. Sometimes changing your mindset about your failures might be all you need to start getting the right results. Dwelling on failures will only lead you to self-pity, and self-pity will in turn drain you of the much-needed motivation you need to keep trying.

- **Try harder and work smarter:** You can increase the time you spend trying to internalize any particular habit or the time you spend trying to achieve your daily goals. This can only be possible by looking at your daily To-do list to see where you can cut down on time and what you can eliminate. It will also help you to adopt new approaches or refine the one you have been using. Learn new tips and tricks that others around you use to go through with their daily goals and fix them where they fit into your own plans and routines.

- **Persevere:** Do not stop when and where you fail. Quitting is never in the success equation. If you refuse to quit, soon you will look back and be glad you never gave up when you faced setbacks and challenges.

Follow the habit blueprint resource below to put everything you have learnt in this book into immediate action.

Step 15: Take Immediate Action Using the Habit Blueprint Resource

To sum it all up and to help you make daily progress with your habit, here are some steps you can take:

1: Make your habit change a success by picking a keystone habit in every area of your life

We talked about the power of <u>keystone habits</u> as well as how they can help you build several other positive habits. About 50% of everything you do daily happens without your conscious participation. This is because these habits are on autopilot and can happen subconsciously. More than half of your daily behaviors happen automatically, and it does not matter whether they are good or bad habits.

Consciously choosing and internalizing a keystone habit will help you cause a good ripple effect and support the building of positive behaviors. Some common keystone habits you can begin with include exercise, sleep, eating right, spending less, etc.

2: Make your first steps unbelievably small

This will help you remove the problem of lack of willpower, which stops most people from changing their habits. It is easy to fail when you try to make big lifestyle changes excessively fast. Such huge attempts fail because your willpower tends to fluctuate unpredictably all through the day, with several factors being responsible for inducing negative fluctuations.

Instead of trying to turn into a marathon guru in one day, read a whole book all at once, or change your eating habit right away; you can set a goal to run only 5 minutes every day, eat a single apple every day, or read one page of the book you wish to read.

Anyone can run for minutes, eat an apple a day, read a page of any book. The good thing about starting small is that it is very unlikely that you will stop after the one page, 5 minutes run, or on apple.

3: Have visual reminders and triggers placed around you

Every habit, whether negative or positive, has a cue. You can help your new positive habits stick by placing visual reminders and triggers all around you. For instance, if you are working or building a new habit of working out first thing every morning, you can place your workout kit next to your bed to ensure you see it immediately after you wake each morning. This will trigger you to put them on and hit the road.

4: Set an alarm or timer on your calendar whenever you need to engage in that new habit or behavior

Setting an alarm will help you wake up when you should and engage in your daily habits, especially when you are working on building new habits. Having a specific time to engage in certain activities such as your mindful meditation and physical workouts will help you stick to your habits and engage in them daily.

5: Give yourself time to master the new habits

You will make mistakes; there is no doubt about that. Your attempts will yield results sometimes, and fail sometimes. It is important you give yourself time and keep trying until your new habits form.

6: Change your strategies if they are not yielding the right results

If the steps you have been taking are not working, you need to stop and look at your habits and strategies once more to know when to make amendments and adopt new strategies.

7: Use the power of rewards lavishly

When it comes to building habits, rewards are so powerful that they can help you stick to any new behavior. Choose a reward that you will consider worth earning and one that can motivate you enough to pursue your daily goals and follow your habits.

Conclusion

Building new habits is not easy. However, with the right efforts and approaches, you can succeed at changing your life and daily routines by replacing your negative habits with positive ones.

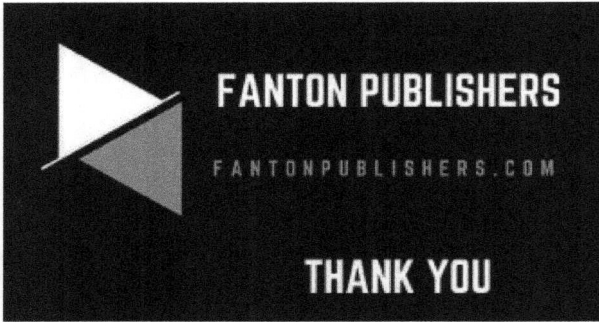

Do You Like My Book & Approach To Publishing?

If you like my writing and style and would love the ease of learning literally everything you can get your hands on from Fantonpublishers.com, I'd really need you to do me either of the following favors.

1: First, I'd Love It If You Leave a Review of This Book on Amazon.

2: Grab Some Freebies On Your Way Out; Giving Is Receiving, Right?

I gave you a complimentary book at the start of the book. If you are still interested, grab it here.

5 Pillar Life Transformation Checklist: http://bit.ly/2fantonfreebie

3: Stay tuned for my next book.

PSS: Let Me Also Help You Save Some Money!

If you are a heavy reader, have you considered subscribing to Kindle Unlimited? You can read this and millions of other books for just $9.99 a month)! You can check it out by searching for Kindle Unlimited on Amazon!

www.ingramcontent.com/pod-product-compliance
Lightning Source LLC
Chambersburg PA
CBHW031134020426
42333CB00012B/377